THIS WOMAN REVEALED

POETRY BY AN AFRICAN WOMAN

Miss Hannah H. Tarindwa

i

Published 2014 by Fairfield Press, Middlesbrough

ISBN: 978-1-908690-26-5

This Woman Revealed

May the Lord Bless you

And protect you

May the Lord smile on you

And be gracious to you

May the Lord show you his favour

And give you peace

Priestly Blessing

-Numbers 6:24-26

Preface

Ever so often, as the saying goes, there comes that gem of literary talent that makes you sit up and notice. Miss Hannah H. Tarindwa is that gem. We have seen several female voices emerge on the Zimbabwean literary landscape recently, and there is plenty of room for more. But here is a writer who encapsulates all that is delightful and exciting about the work of the Zimbabwean female writer.

Can Tarindwa's poetry be compared to the work of a male writer? Most definitely. But that is not what she is doing here. As the title states quite succinctly, this anthology is the voice of a woman, *this* woman.

It has been a pleasure and huge honour to be part of this undertaking. And now, dear reader, you are part of it too. Thank you very much, Hannah, for sharing.

Masimba Musodza, Middlesbrough

Dedication

This collection I dedicate to the most important woman in my life, my mother, Grace Anne Upenyu Tambo. A lot of who I am today is her.

Acknowledgements

I would like to acknowledge the gift of literacy and then the gift of being a scribe given to me by God the creator of heaven and earth, whom I believe held my hand through the writing of many of these poems

A special thank you goes to the editor Barbara Mhangami-Ruwende who saw the need for perfection and offered herself to the time-consuming and tiring task of editing despite her other commitments. She walked ten extra miles for this book. You are one of the few people who leave me speechless! I love you sis.

It would have been impossible for me to have the courage alone to finally put these poems together without the instating voice of my friend since teenage-hood, Tendayi Mkondo. Thank you, Tee. This is true also of Thenjiwe S. Ziwenga who reminded me that talents are useless unless they are shown.

Thank you Masimba Musodza and Fairfield Author Services for the discussions and priceless advice on how to get the book out to the masses. I will never again be 'mousy'.

To all my English teachers, particularly Sr. Jovita (Dominican O.P) who showed me how to write poetry intellectually and still express my emotions clearly, a great big thank you. To all the friends and family who loved me even though they did not always understand me, thank you for that love and your presence.

To you, reading this book of poetry in the 21st Century.... Thank you for keeping poetry alive and allowing me to speak to you in your private space.

The Poetry Within

This Skin

In this skin is happiness,
She mixes and mingles with confidence
They dance and dine with self- respect
A wholeness that comes from life's experiences
The tears come, no longer with embarrassment
The laughter roars unashamedly
Pleasure and pain give each other space and time
For they are me: They are within this skin

Once, it felt wrong to be me,
This one and that one decided what I was to be
It was not an easy feat;
Longing and trying to please
But no longer do I put them first.
I did it by putting up a ferocious fight.
And discovered with each trial, tribulation and mistake,
My best friend was not outside but within.

Regrets, wishes, hopes and dreams, tormented me
They came; some stayed, and most of them left
Yet here I stand ready to face the next stage of my life
My spirit was shaken but never broken
My skin is still soft, gentle, smooth and beautiful to touch
I live in this skin that is not be pain-proof
It has given me my identity:
Each wound and scar, present and past,
Makes me glad it is my skin.

Sex is one of the most interesting things we humans have to play with, and we've reduced it to polyester underpants and implants. We are selling ourselves unbelievably short

- Ariel Levy, Female Chauvinist Pigs: Women and the Rise of Raunch Culture.

Moment of Pleasure

It burned; the passion within- The sweat

What mattered was the heartbeat,

Each as fast as the other

Longing for fulfilment

There was a feathery touch and then a sensuous squeeze

A sudden release ushering in - welcome relief

So much more than anticipated,

Intensity of the highest kind

Quivering the head to the little toe

Not a need but a powerful want

The lingering essence was overwhelming

Pulling one into the other passionately

Day by day, set aside but not ignored

Acknowledged

But never fulfilled...

Until this moment of pleasure

The White Shirt

The sweeping sounds of the ocean's ebb and flow surround us
Simple and complex words melt
Giving way to the energies of our two spirits
The light around us illuminates our eyes and our skins radiate
It blankets us in reassuring warmth.
Your tender and powerful mesmerizing smile
Catches my coy smile in the semi-darkness
The softness of the carpet below our feet
Evokes the softness of our embrace
I stare at your body; naked,
Save for the boxers that cover your centre
You return the compliment my body trembles under your stare
Embraced only by your crisp white shirt,
Barely revealing the lace lingerie beneath it.
My feet are adorned by a sleek pair of black and silver heels.
Your stare penetrates me,
Stepping towards you, slowly,
My mind empty of all else but this moment
As slowly as I walk towards you,
Your lips part in delight
Both of us need not to speak now
We just listen to the continuous ebb and flow
The sea is the symphony
And we will complement it with a dance.

The White shirt 2

Our dance is harmonious,
No hurry, no hushes, no setbacks, no limitations.
I get close to you
And remove my heels one at a time, watching you
Your arms stretch out to me
And your palms caress my soft cheeks gently.
Softly they slide down to the front of the shirt
One by one, you unbutton it,
It rustles to the floor like a dead leaf in the autumn wind
My skin vibrates
Blood simmers under my skin
My heart races, beating against my ribs
I am secure in your empowering presence
And you are confident in my consuming presence
No doubts, no second thoughts, no regrets,
It is in this moment we really see each other—
You are mine as much as I am yours.
Only in this moment
An almost celestial union occurs
As if this was meant to be from the beginning of creation.
The rest if the world fades
We mingle in each other's skin
Our scents unify, our breaths, our inner beings
I reveal my nakedness to you.

Feel Good

Make me feel good,
Caress my ears with your honeyed words
Tell me sweet 'some-things',
That will make me glad when I am alone.

Make me feel good
Whether it is just for this moment
Or for all eternity to come
Do something, say something; anything!

Make me feel good
No matter whether truth or lie
Just give me sweet escape;
To a world that could be or is.
Make me feel good
I have given you the power to do so
Your tongue and your hands dispensing pleasure
Just for me!

Make me feel good
In a way that is sweetly subtle
Then I will be ecstatic
My nerves fully awake.

Make me feel good
You know how, you have done it before
Do it again, like the expert you are
With me in your hands like soft putty
Make me feel good
Embrace me with sweet memories
That I will one day seek
When alone, once again, I shall find myself.

When I Get Sleepy

When I get sleepy
I feel so sexy
My nerves are on the edge
Extra ticklish
Yet longing for touch

When I get sleepy
I feel so ready
Like a ripe fruit ready to be eaten
Filled with sweet juices
To bring nourishment and satiation

When I get sleepy
I feel like being caressed
On all my woman parts
On the tips of my mountains
And to the depths of my valleys.

A woman is a flower in a garden;
Her husband is the fence around it.

-Proverb from Ghana

Bells Around

The feeling, felt once or twice

Bells around ring, arousing all senses to life!

The skin and every nerve vibrates with life

The ears hear songs of angels

There is the smell of spring all year round

The taste is so sweet it can be overwhelming

Everything looks brilliant! Like a shimmering light is cast on them

All senses are elevated

Bells of love are around

They ring melodiously everywhere

Giving a sense of peace and serenity

There is harmony in the bells around

And the melody brings my whole being to dancing

The bells around ring and let the world see

He Loves Her

He says it, he shows it,

As they walk he picks a yellow flower for her

He does not know its name

But he likes how it makes her smile

That has him longing to pull her close to him, to embrace her

So that her soft breasts gently squeeze on his firm chest

It is not a game of seduction

It is a manner of celebrating love

He looks into her brown, sincere eyes and he finds rest

Calm that he cannot comprehend pulls him into her world.

Her afro her and smooth hazel brown skin

Dotted on the forehead, a few black spots

Her nose a well-placed button in the middle of her longish, yet round face

He thinks: the creator took His time here

Making lips that have a perfect mid –dent on the upper lip and fullness on the lower lip

They are slightly pink-brow kissable lips,

He stares as she speaks

Her body is short and voluptuously rotund

Breasts well formed, the perfect bosom for him

Her waist compliments her hips and thighs

Covered beneath the white floral skirt which is spread out

Like a princess dress

Captivated in her aura as if under a spell

He listens and responds surrounded by a wild fire of passion for her

He loves her, her mannerisms

The way she scratches her nose when she is absent minded

Or chews her lower lip when concentrating

All about her captivates him

Let Us Chat.

Today tell me; please
What do you want us to talk about?
That would make us remember each other?
A conversation we will each recall
Alone in a crowd we will smile
Thinking of what we shall speak of now.
Oh do tell me, I beg.

What will excite both of us?
Something that will get us lost in time
Be surprised to hear the early morning birds chirping
To be amazed hearing the friendly neighbour's greeting;
"Good morning, how did you sleep?"
I would like to have *that* chat with you.

Such that the words we exchange we shall treasure
That when one day I may see a different face of yours
A face that may be filled with tension and anger towards me
I will harken back to today, to this exchange
And I will know then as I know now
That I have a piece of you in me
In a conversation of what you and I both like

<u>Once upon an African Winter Night</u>

In the midst of the cold African night

How I miss my African man

He holds me close and chases the night cold away

But now he is not here,

He is away from me tonight

Taken a bus to a place so many kilometres away

He is not neglecting me

He is gone away for me

Working for me, for him, for them, for us

He is not away for long, a few days and he will return

I will be warm again, inside and out

When my African man returns to his African woman

To chase this African cold away

THE DOOR IS OPEN

The shy knock echoes into the room

No answer.

The knock gets bolder and louder

Still

No answer.

There is no lock though, no restriction

A creek

It swings slightly; opening

Invitingly

The door is open:

Enter

Let not fear grip you

Overcome it

The door is open:

Enter

Despite what you have heard before

Conquer!

Don't wait a second longer

The door is open!

Enter!

WARS WERE STARTED FOR LESS

Wars have been started for less
I would start one for him, for he is mine
Your deceptive eyes do not bother me
For I know that he prefers my sexy ones.
Your lips would not lure him to you
For mine are more juicy and sweet.

Wars have been started for less
So love is a noble cause, I will be justified
I give you not empty threats,
Do not provoke the craziness I carry within
I will tear you to pieces
Ruthlessly like a lioness scorned.
Oh my, oh my dear woman
Do not dare to even look at him
Forget the man: he is mine.

Wars have been started for less
He will be my cause and the war will be bitter and cold
I am not threatened by your hips
For they do not seduce him as mine have
I know that venomous words drip from your tongue
Like poison, you may speak to him and bring death to us
But I will have battle scars first
Than to ever let you get that far.

Wars have been started for less
A war for my man would be aptly justified

NEVER BE AFRAID TO
RAISE YOUR VOICE FOR
HONESTY AND TRUTH AND
COMPASSION AGAINST
INJUSTICE AND LYING AND
GREED. IF PEOPLE ALL OVER
THE WORLD WOULD DO
THIS, IT WOULD CHANGE
THE EARTH.

— WILLIAM FAULKNER

Silenced

Silenced by fear
Silenced by threats
Speech limited is thought truncated
If what is, IS
Why then, why can it not be spoken?

Words stifled in the throat
To keep the open secret, secret
For fear of offending
Revelations of truth
Best kept underground
Or in chains, behind bars.

Silenced by those that are more equal
Gagged by strength of influence
And pockets heavy with ill-gotten gold
The poor dare not speak or squeak
For though they have nothing
They surely have more to lose.

Rabid Hunger

Why are you so hungry for battles and wars?

How come you are so thirsty for boiling blood?

Who told you death was the best retribution against a foe?

Is this what they taught you when you were but a lad?

Does it rest your busy and crowded mind?

To think you have taken a mother, an aunt, a sister?

Is it an insane type of hatred that makes you so horridly blind?

To snuff out the life of a father, an uncle, a brother?

It forever baffles, vexes and troubles me deeply

Why people (you call them soldiers) must die, bleed, be

mutilated.

Is it the method that is meant to be?

When it is over, distant cries of mourning are heard,

Whilst others ululate, in gory jubilation

Your hunger remains rabid still

For you send out others to the fields

To plough dead bodies for you

They choose to die at your command

For patriotism which we all know is not real.

Rent to Rent

Living from rent to rent
Praying for the monthly miracle to be sent
Nothing can be planned or wished for
Now and here is all there is; nowhere to go.
At times you wish you could have an interview with death
To know when they will come to lay your wreath
For all you live for is simple survival
Your soul just there; desperately needs revival
Everything seems to need that breathe of life
It has been a while since you felt alive.
Money becomes the enemy you must need
To pay bills, get by, not because of greed.
Abilities, talent, a willing body you have
So why does it seem like you are waiting for a save?
On your knees then, to cry and pray
Else in search of more than rent you may fall astray.
Living from rent to bitter rent,
Earnestly praying for the monthly miracle to be sent!

Let Me

Let me sing, dance and ululate all day
Give me ground to be joyful, calm and crazy!
Have me enjoy the sound of *hosho* and hand beaten drums
Let me be fearless, free and content

For soon there will be no song,
No beat in my feet or saliva to ululate
No joy to enjoy, just conflict and madness.
I will have to endure the sound of the distant gunshots
And terrible pain-filled screams thereafter.
I will be fear-filled, trapped and unsatisfied.

Let me watch the clear showing stars at night
And the beautiful wisps of clouds by day
As I feel the warmth of the tender embrace
Of true love and acceptance.

I long to walk the streets with genuine smiles
And comfortably familiar faces.
To be the good neighbour and reliable friend

Yet a reddish smoke fills my skies
By night and by day
The air suffocates me with its polluted clasp of rejection
On the streets it is mistrust and frowns
Every face a suspect against my self-preservation.

Humans must have sometime walked this earth
Now vessels of hate and mistrust roam on it.
We have stripped each other mercilessly
Of things that matter truly
Dressing others in a million dollar bills
While others without go about naked.

"If you think anyone is sane you just don't know enough about them."

— Christopher Moore, *Practical Demon-keeping*

You Know Me Not

You have no idea who I am

So say nothing of what I am to be

Ignorance drives you against me

Pure pity drives me far from you.

Sadder still as I watch you watching me

So involved in wanting to see me fall

Must make you sick to watch me rise!

Shame on you

Good for me.

I smile at your smirk

Laugh at you miserable frown

Pathetically hoping for the worst

Yet watching me get the best…

You know nothing of who I am

So say nothing of who I am to be.

The Woman

Standing over his trembling body

Axe in hand

Something about him smelt mouldy

This time, she would defend herself.

When last did he say a word gentle or kind?

She stared at him now with no fear.

All he had ever done was get her from behind.

Today she felt no sweat, nor tear.

Time had come when it would all end;

He had to suffer for making her this way.

Long nights and hard days she had spent

Only for him to take her sanity away.

From nowhere a voice she knew called out,

The man and the axe disappeared.

She looked around, confused, feeling the urge to shriek!!

From the dream she wakes and he appears:

"Lazy woman get my axe, get out of bed!!

Do you hear? I will chop of your head, stupid!"

WOMAN AT THE BENCH
(Vessel of malice)

As she sat on the park bench

All was far from well;

Her mind was not at peace

But her smile did not betray that

They passed her, nodded at her

Others even admired and envied her

She looked, at best, the calmest woman ever

But inside a storm brewed

A madness grew darker and darker

Consuming the light she might have had

She sat there on the park bench

As if waiting for a sign.

No one could have guessed or seen

The poison she created and harboured

Deep within her it festered.

Hate only, fed the venom within.

Un-forgiveness made it more lethal.

But there she sat on the park bench

Smiling to them gently as they smiled back

If only they looked closer into her eyes

They would not have smiled back

As an evil fire burnt the tears away

There were no more genuine emotions

She was just a vessel of malice

Pain and thoughts of vengeance filled her

She could not feel remorse

It had been swallowed by the venom

Joy, laughter, gentleness, sweetness

Were not of her being anymore

Just a deep black void was left there

It settled and made her its home.

She stood up; took a deep breath

Walked slowly eastbound.

Thursday afternoon was through now

She was returning to the dungeon she called home

Returning to the enemies she called family

To the self she hated,

Next Thursday she would return to the bench

To give fake smiles to familiar strangers

Whilst imagining the life she never had

And cooled off from the life that was really hers

To imagine herself elsewhere, free

Knowing well that being alive and being free

Were never to occur at once

She walked eastbound

She did not turn to bid farewell to the bench

The only place where she found solitude

The bench: Her only true friend and solace

Wasted

My shoes, where are my damn shoes?!
Stumbling out, walking bare foot
Yes you know who I am,

My shoes, where are those damned heels
Tripping out, walking naked on my feet
Yes you know who I am, you know my name

And hell...yes bloody hell
And hell I know and you know what I am
Yes I am an alcoholic
How does that affect you?
Does it offend and disgust you?
Do you feel shame on my behalf?
A woman of such high standing
Burping, cursing, kicking things out of my way
Scratching my behind in an un-lady like manner
Shouting obscenities for the late coming of my drink!

Are you utterly at loss for words?
When you behold me dancing unreservedly
Throwing every morsel of caution to the wind
Stop staring! Else you will be next
Oh yes, on my list of offenses you may go.
Give me my shoes now
Let me stumble, waddle and burp rudely
On my way out, getting to my home
I need my bed,
It's my bad
I am wasted!

The Sunday Act

Up! Up! Up!

We are going to church
Where are our nicest clothes?
The best pair of shoes; not that one!
The newest pair
Not the pair people saw last week!
What will they think of our fashion sense?
Remind us to change our hairstyles
Two Sundays is enough

Lights, Camera, Action!

Do they see us?
Do they hear us bellowing praise and worship?
Are our voices wowing them?
We will raise our hands as high as we can
They must admire us; see us as prayer warriors.

Phew, it is done now...
Off with those wretched heels and tight ties
We have done what needs to be done
We can finally hang up our hair!

Switch off, please; no lights, no cameras, no action here!

See you next Sunday.

*Matthew 6:5

Guilt-Ridden

You can barely look at her

Your guilt eats at you...

What have you done?

Why did you do it?

It felt like some game then

Like a passing phase

But she did something to you

She is also unaware of what she did to you

Her teary eyes, tearful for you

Send icy cold shivers all over your being

What have you done?

Was it all worth the lies?

The temporary feeling of elevation

Does not feel so freeing now; does it?

As you now sink deeper and deeper in guilt.

The Anticipated Dream

In the hustle and bustle of everyday life

We wonder into strange places

Some, not the best for us

Others more appropriate.

We search with unwavering attention

For acceptance and love

We anticipate that fairy tale dream come true

Hoping every minute that it is possible

(Untitled)

How do you get rid of a thought?

Thoughts, wishes and hopes society says you must not have

How do you strengthen your inner-self?

To suppress an emotion unreciprocated

How do you settle your heart?

Remind it one more time of a time it beat rhythmically like this

Only to be put into discord and shattered

Remind it of when the darkest depression set in

When appetite became a stranger

Tears, the companion of the day

When the world lost its colour

The rays of the sun brought no comfort

All around it was cold

Ears lost the ability to hear

Eyes could only stare blankly into the abyss of days to come

Is that how you get rid of any thought of love?

I should think it effective to do so

Money and corruption are ruining the land, crooked politicians betray the working man, pocketing the profits and treating us like sheep, and we're tired of hearing promises that we know they'll never keep.

-Ray Davies

The Devil Wears A Suit And Tie

The devil wears a suit and tie
And he seduced me.
Sweetly whispering lies into my ears;
But it didn't seem so bad then
Actually it felt like he genuinely cared for me!
Besides he said it would only cost an X.
He would bring me joy,
He would bring me comfort
He would provide for me and protect me
He said my life would be happier;
That I would get all the things that I wanted;
That he would deliver ALL I needed.
It was all about me!
I was his main concern and he lived just for me!

All it took would be a few minutes
(Or hours –as written in the small print)
Of my time
A dip of my little finger in proof ink
And the oh-so-important-X

So, seduced and entranced by charm, humour and a free t-shirt
I made the choice, he was THE man!
I liked how he made me believe in his extra-terrestrial promises
I saw myself there where I wanted to be!
I couldn't keep such good news to myself
I told anyone and everyone about MY man
They had to make him theirs too,
If things were going to be right!
And I got annoyed and frustrated with those who chose not to
believe
Or those who preferred another devil who spoke in a different
manner
Damn them…
I was seduced and I didn't need any more convincing

I slept early, preparing myself
I dreamt of the Promised Land he spoke of
Geared up, I would support his cause
He had said it was all about me after all
Anxiety filled me, the anticipation, intoxicating
And then finally the day came...
Excitement to play my part
To exercising my right! Shivers of eagerness filled me
I got to the queue early, but I was not alone
His words had seduced many; all of us
Jacketed, scarfed, woolly hats, gloves, and a lit fire
Braved the cold that hit our cheeks hard
But the fire of desire warmed us from within.

Did I know that he would be sleeping comfortably?
Covered by imported winter sheets
And the heavy oriental blankets
Couture bedding fit for kings and important people
He had not even woken up to wear his suit and tie.
Even when he eventually did wake up,
He would be treated to hot milk in his oats
Or cereal of choice according to what he did not have yesterday
And would not have tomorrow
My stomach grumbled but that was ok,
I was used to that sound now
"I ought to be less greedy," I warned myself.
My turn came, after a not-so-long
Three hour wait
I returned home satisfied and feeling accomplished.
The power was gone... oh but soon that will be a thing of the
past
I took a bucket to fill it as the water was trickling its last drops of
the day
My seducer had told me these were the works of detractors
They were there all around us
Wishing ill upon us, enemies I did not see directly
But he saw them clearly
And he would put an end to their attacks on my daily bread.

He would ward them off and help me provide for myself
adequately
The day to pay X's came and went.
Days came and went, just as the power came and went
Though the power went more than it came
The water made my stomach turn,
Oh, that is when I did not have to go next door to borrow from
their well
When the brown and blackish water
Trickled from the tap
Silently I wished I could afford a filter…
Then I thought...
Oh yes my seducer is fighting for me somewhere
I am sure he remembers me when he has his borehole and
filtered water
His power does not go off, of course
That would be ridiculous, as he is the warrior for my cause
That's what he told me, I remember as I stare at the dwindling
candle
But as the candle melts away and fades
A bright light shines in my mind
Opening my eyes to my folly and gullibility
The devil did not speak to me
He spoke to the crowd which I was part of
And his shining suit blew me away,
Matching with his well-tied tie
Way before words of deception flowed effortlessly from between
his lips
I was played for a fool
Sold my X for his betterment
Stagnant I remain, if I do not sink deeper in the muddy pit
Where he spoke to me though he stood on elevated polished
ground

I snap out of the trance I had been induced
It is too late
In anger I kick the stones on the path to fetch firewood
Long ago the city was the place where electricity flowed
Now smoke from household cooking fires
Mingles with the dust in the air
Tongues click and cluck in helpless resentment
All have been duped
The devil surely wears a tie and a suit.

You care nothing for me

No, no, no, no, no
I refused for it is too hard to believe
Even now as I see it, I know what I know
There is no change as long as I live
Well… maybe a slight change
But only in faces and placement of words
The meaning is in the same range.
Different wars, at different times but the same ammunition.

Promises dished out so frivolously
Carelessly thrown like mush to a bunch of pigs!
Promises of change towards honesty
Yet in secret they congregate in diabolical leagues.
I shake my head in pity, watch and walk on by.
I am even given rights to participate in such!
Oh please!!!
Give me something money can buy
Time ticks away; this is reality.

I have come to know and detest you
I know what you really stand for
I am never on your mind
You do not know me, nor do you care for me
I am just a face in the crowd…just a statistic
I belong to the sad ninety-five percent*, fighting
Doing all I can do for my survival.

They say my words are powerful
And warn that I should guard my tongue.
They say that speech must be thought out
To prepare the words I wish to share.
Yet when I speak out good and out loud wish it
Nothing of it comes to life and lives
You have shut all gates for me
All I do is stand, watch and let you be.

*95%- refers to the 2013 statistics of the formally unemployed in Zimbabwe

Rumours

Oh, did you hear about so and so?
Oh everyone knew that long back!
Oh she didn't know?
It was common knowledge!
It was a rumour though,
It was said via the grapevine
People speculated, and someone made it reality
Horrid and filthy those made up words can be
They may stem slowly as a practical joke
Or out of malice for revenge
Or even fear of the unknown.

Rumours have been known to break up homes
To split families that were stable and happy
They have been known to shake economies
And worst of all to start wars that end the lives of innocence

The venom in three words, "did you hear?"
Poisons all who are touched by it
Leaving only,
A cacophony of clanging empty vessels

"Oh, he must have said it, who else would?"
"Maybe he did maybe he did not,
But I am betting he probably did"
Acidic words of uncertainty formulated
To entertain
Yet the trail of destruction that follows is vile
No one is immune
We are all culprits and all are victims!

"It's never ok to hit a girl. NEVER. Not even if she cheats on you. A girl is not your property. She's a human being. She is just as important as you. She is your equal. And her wishes and feelings are just as valid as yours. All you can do is treat her nice, and hope she wants to be with you. If she chooses to be with you, great! If not, or if she chooses to leave you at some point, you have to let her go. You have no right to stop her. You don't own her, and you don't have the right to tell her what to do. She's your partner.

Not your servant, not your sex slave, and not your punching bag."

— Oliver Markus, *Sex and Crime: Oliver's Strange Journey*

Hmm... To The Cheater

Ready to cheat on what is yours

Eager to please what is does not belong to you

You pla the fool today

To say it was an error tomorrow

(Yeah right!)

How is it the sweet things done today?

Turn to silliness or become mundane tomorrow

Binding promises and oaths of today that bind

Become null and void as soon as the new sun rises?

How was your night, my love?

Sweetheart, did you dream of me?

What did you eat for lunch, darling?

Words of care and endearment lost

To the familiarity that breeds contempt

Why should events that brought joy and warmth change?

It becomes an offense for the victim of circumstance to ask;

"Why have you changed these days?"

When You Remember Me

I wish when you remember me
You see an ever smiling and cheerful face
You hear the echo of joyful child-like laughter
You remember the silky feel of my skin
You smell the lingering of my signature sweet perfume

I do not wish you to remember
The tears I wept bitterly in sorrow and anguish
The sound of my wailing and pleas
How my skin became as hard as a fortress
At the bitter taste of rejection

I wish that you only recall the good and that only
And that your mind revokes all the bad
Because my intentions were only to be right
Yet things kept going and turning out wrong
The situation refused to change, now fortified in history.

The Hidden Night

There was thunder
But no rain
There must have been lightning
But it was unseen
Well not in that vicinity
There was pain in that dark night
There was anger and resentment.
Emotions ran high
And a lot of love was lost
Not just a lot, all of it
The pain was physical: slap after slap
It was mental: was this really happening?
It was spiritual: Where was my God?

There was more and more thunder
Yet still no rain
Why was I thinking of the weather
When I had a monster stomping on me
I saw something deeper than hate
Questioned if that was the person I knew
Questions popped into and out of me
My skin had never felt such torture
He paused, What for?
Was he tired?

The thunder finally stopped
And the rain started
My tears flowed
Bringing strength from somewhere unknown

I stood up to run and escape fate
But was grabbed in my tracks
Found myself again on the cold floor
Saw ants rushing from me,
Free ants, another strange thought in and out of my head.

Now there is no thunder at all
No rain, falling or anticipated
All is well and I am not there
I left and set myself free
Years passed, but not the memory
I remembered painfully but never shared
The one thing I knew to do
So as not to hurt again
Was to keep that night hidden;
That dreadful night; hidden in my memory.

Bitter Escape

I looked back from a distance
I had run as far as I could
Turning only when I felt I would not make a U-turn
It had to be done
You made it difficult
I tried my best many times
Plotting and scheming methods and correct timing
But it was never to be
'Til in that moment I decided it had to be done
There where you are, I longed to be
There, I stayed and felt comfortable,
You were so familiar
But it was nothing that would benefit me
For in your presence was deep darkness
That sapped the brightness out of me.
I did not remember the last time I had laughed
There was no sound of music.
No feet danced and bodies were stiff
Your presence was a shadow,
Forever blocking the sun from a beautiful garden
Bringing doom and curbing growth.
Sapping colour leaving only grey and rot
I ran and cried, wondering why I felt pain
The escape felt bitter, the freedom a let-down
Had your claws become an embrace?
It was a sorrowful escape, like a child running from its beloved
mother
Yet it was the best choice I ever made
I turned back to look but not for long
Fear of turning into a salt pillar urged me on!

"A daughter without her mother is a woman broken. It is a loss that turns to arthritis and settles deep into her bones."
— Kristin Hannah, *Summer Island*

I did not Know You

I did not know you,
So I have come to know
I thought I had you figured out,
That the story was simple and straight forward
But alas it is not so!
For there you sailed in tougher storms than I had seen
You walked in hotter deserts than I felt
My God, what pain did you suffer?
How many nights did you, like me, weep?
The bottle turned out to be your best friend too

I did not know you
So I have come to know
But I became you without knowing it
A few details, here and there changed
Yet the cuts and bruises close to identical
They need no DNA test to show I am yours
I have become a replica with my sad lifestyle
It happened, without my knowledge
Yet I questioned constantly
How would you feel to see me now?

I did not know you
So I have come to know
But I always admired you greatly
You took me as I am and gave me more than I knew
You even gave me more than you knew
The good, the bad and the ugliest of me, you gave
It may be delayed knowledge now
But now when I see you in my mirror I get it,
I understand why so much of me *is* you
There was no way I could have been any different.

Seventeen years

Seventeen years on and I am still lost

Seventeen years on and I am needing you even more!
Did not some old wise person mention
That time heals all wounds?
So why does time continue
To dig deeper on the wound you left?
Maybe we know different times, them and I.
Nothing I do seems quite proper
Nothing I touch really prospers.
You truly were my foundation and pillar
Why did The Creator take you and leave me behind?

Seventeen years on and this is still my desire.

Seventeen years on no answer has come to me yet.
To be free of the complexities I face
As clearly I am not handling them well
You left me clueless and alone
The success you saw remains still a vision
I grew, yet I am still no one with nothing but struggle
Abrupt decisions are the core of my existence
Certainly not the woman I saw myself to be
Things just unravel before me.

Seventeen years on and I write to you

Seventeen years on, wishing you could come to read
Poetry ever written in tear-oceans
Pain anguish, longing and more longing
Will you not come back to get me?

Grace, dearest Grace, put in a word for me
The angel of life has no reason to ignore me
What do I do on this here earth?
Who am I to anyone?
Am I not just another time pusher?
Seventeen years on and I am listening hard

Seventeen years on and I cannot hear your voice.
Sing to me like you did before
Run your fingers through my hair with love
Tell me when we will be together again, I beg
I am not handling this world well without you
Seventeen years on.

Why her?

When I die I shall be alone

The "fond" memories of me will soon fade

I will not be anyone's last thought as they lie in bed

When I die not many will weep

The few that will cry will not suffer much

For I have not much to leave behind for them

In fact I have nothing really

Eighteen years ago since she left me

I wondered; why her not me?

What value am I to the world, to anyone?

I was sure God had struck his heavy hand wrongly

Had he missed or was this what others had spoken of?

The horrid sense of humour to inflict on a child?

Eighteen years later still no companion

And the question lingers; "Why her?"

One day, Some Day

Sweat, blood and tears

The goal to have good years

The world will hurt me and leave bruises

I go on not wanting to be one who snoozes

The world threw sticks and stones

They caused pain, but did not break my bones!

I was for the better, for the best

My mind and body not knowing rest.

I have to make it, I do not have a choice

I might not even get the chance to drive a Rolls Royce

But I want to look back and smile

Saying, 'well done, I walked the extra mile!

Have you ever been in love? Horrible isn't it? It makes you so vulnerable. It opens your chest and it opens up your heart and it means that someone can get inside you and mess you up. You build up all these defenses, you build up a whole suit of armour, so that nothing can hurt you, then one stupid person, no different from any other stupid person, wanders into your stupid life.... You give them a piece of you. They didn't ask for it. They did something dumb one day, like kiss you or smile at you, and then your life isn't your own anymore. Love takes hostages. It gets inside you. It eats you out and leaves you crying in the darkness, so simple a phrase like 'maybe we should be just friends' turns into a glass splinter working its way into your heart. It hurts. Not just in the imagination. Not just in the mind. It's a soul-hurt, a real gets-inside-you-and-rips-you-apart pain. I hate love.

~Neil Gaiman, *The Sandman, Vol. 9: The Kindly Ones*

SHOULD I PRETEND?

Should I pretend not to care?
Should I smile on as though I am without a worry?
Be happily single and alone?
Replying falsely at family gatherings:
"I am ok, it will happen in God's time?"

Should I pretend I do not want it too?
The 'loving' husband and 'cutest' baby?
Be proud to be single and working (at least!)
Being the best aunty to everyone else's children

Should I pretend to accept this 'lifestyle of choice'?
To sleep alone on cold nights
To have no one I can rely on and depend on fully
Having an uncle, aunt, a brother or cousin as next of kin

Should I pretend that I go to weddings joyfully
That I am not envious,
I am simply happy for the two of them,
That not a single bone in me wishes I could also have a piece of
that pie

Should I pretend that the single salary is ok?
I am independent and free
That I do not wish to share my responsibilities and my
successes?
That things matter more to me than a human being I call my
own?

Should I pretend not to care?
Whilst fighting back tears of longing
To show outwardly a content woman
Whilst hiding the woman who is wondering; where is the one
man for me?

Foolish

In a world of agony and pain

You did nothing to relieve me of it

Instead you inflicted more of it onto me

Worse still, you did it with steady hands

Unaware of your intentions

I meekly followed my heart

My weak, longing and loving heart

Only to find I followed you into a pit

Not much different from hell.

Tears welled up within me:

Fooled again!

How could a woman be so intelligent?

Yet so damn desperate.

I was in misery, you continued on

Like nothing happened

And all I could do is wonder

How you could be so selfish?

How could I be so foolish?

STUCK

The wheels rolled on and on
But the vehicle did not move
The situation was bleak,
Thunder after lightning, in the hard hitting rain
It would need one of the two to get out and push.

Who would make that sacrifice?
Push and get dirty and wet?
Who would take one for the team?

Both individuals stared at each other
Each expecting the other to do it
Both were stuck
Mentally, physically, spiritually
While one thought the other had to
The other thought that maybe the other would offer.
The situation needed change
That was clearer than the cloudy state they were in.

The question was who would change it?

Poor man, poor woman, pathetic couple
They were stuck!

Once I loved

Once I loved unconditionally
I gave myself unreservedly
Opened gates of trust and loyalty
Loved, honoured and respected.
It was magical
Indeed it was, once upon a time,
Too good to be true,
I wanted the dream to go on
I held on, so it could be real.
Real only when I imagined it
My thoughts would for hours dwell
Dwell on that once upon a time
Yet the intelligent life form in me knew
The wiser being in me understood
To let go was necessary
It was vital, most critical.
I acknowledged that and fathomed
In his silence towards me
In my silence towards him
My mind would wonder off
My mind became curious
Nagging me, daily as I called for sleep
For days, weeks, months
A fear began to grow once more;
Would this be forever?
Forever as you had once promised
Just as I promised you.
But that was just once upon a time
That once when I had loved with all I had.

Shot

I have been shot
The pain is deep and definite
Like concentrated heat on the spot
The bullet is still lodged in my chest; I feel it.
My breath may fail me soon.
I am not quite sure what is happening
I am thinking and then... blank
Between collapsing and consciousness
There is knowledge and ignorance all at once
To respond to this pain could be wise
Should I scream or weep silently
Am I just thinking of these emotions?
Or am I actually expressing them?
Are those around me even aware of this?
Can they see how deeply I have been shot?
Can they see how much I am bleeding?
Is there any evidence at all?
Or have I totally lost it now?
The culprit is there looking at me strangely
Is he enjoying my agony?
I think not as I catch a shadow of agony fluttering across his eyes
I got him too!!
He bleeds as I bleed, from deep inside
We shot each other with terrible bullets
Bullets of passion, lust and intensity
Why they hurt so badly is that it was all secret
So we both bleed internally as the world passes by.

Once Upon ...

Once upon a place that now seems far
Once in a time similar to fairy tale times
She felt love with intense measure
She was carried on a fantasy wave
Of a love was surreal.

As it turned out, it *was* too good to be true.
Once, she made love, like in classic romances
Taken into heavenly realms of satisfaction
Where in this place her lover only, mattered
But when the time came to make the choice
She made the hardest one for her
Though it seemed to all like the easiest one
It was truly all or nothing at all
She needed all of him not half of him
He had made mistakes he had to correct
She could not wait or be the other woman.

All that remains now are sweet words
And pictures in her mind that do not want to disappear
Sadder still she does not want them to fade
From that once upon a place and time
When she was subdued by love
Was her love conditional and selfish?
Once upon, she was fleetingly happy
Now she lives with her noble decision
Now, though sad and miserable
She can say she was noble, but miserable

Self-Deception

Lied to myself

Deceived my senses

Went back to a lost self

Had forgotten why that self was lost

She was open and vulnerable

Her senses were incomplete or reliable

Finding her took me back to a time

Brought back familiar feelings that hurt

And feelings that broke me apart

Emotions too overwhelming to contain Anger at self

Regret at the situation

Confusion from the disillusion

Pain vortexing through my core

All I can do is what I have done in the past

Burrow into myself

What made me forget so easily,

That the nature of a man is entwined in lies and deception?

What made me trust him?

I should have known better!

"It is necessary ... for a man <woman, too> to go away by himself< herself> ... to sit on a rock ... and ask, 'Who am I, where have I been, and where am I going?"

— Carl Sandburg

The Foot Soldier's Cry

If life is a battlefield

Then I am a foot soldier,

Trudging on in the battlefield.

I am not a general who hears the distant blasts of fire and

grenades.

I do not see the smoke from a distance.

I do not imagine how things are

And wait for a status report

So that I can issue the next commands

That is not me.

I am the foot soldier

I am the one coughing out smoke-stinking phlegm and blood.

I feel the blasts with every nerve cell;

I no longer hear them.

There is an incessant throbbing of my eardrums

As they pulsate to the bombs and their echoes It used to annoy

me greatly;

Now it is white sound blending with the rush of blood

Flowing through my tense veins

Me, the foot soldier

And I am not the brave type.

I am the fearful type, with the brave face.

Yet I quiver and shake in my tight boots

Nothing I wear for the war fits right.

You see, life is not a choice

Many a time I feel I have few real choices

I am in this battlefield without real weapons

There was no colonel to tell me what to expect

No camouflage to wear so I can blend in.

I feel like I am wearing a white silk gown

Trudging in the middle of a muddy field

Now stained and ugly I just want it off me!

This battle field is hard and my feet walk heavily through

Tears leave murky streaks on my cheeks

Anguish is thudding in my chest.

Surely, life is a battlefield and I am a foot soldier.

PRAYER- TO BE LIKE SALMON

Lord Make me like the salmon

Swimming hard and strong against the tide

Focused on the goal day and night

Never giving up, never tiring.

No Other

I pour out my spirit, my anguish

With a combination of words that come to me

They give me an escape from it.

By giving me insight from the inner being

There is no other way but this

Only this brings real relief

To be open and so vulnerable I can be

Between the electricity in my head

The muscle in my right arm

And the grip of the pen between the index and the thumb

Then the ink

Becomes alive in the letters, the words

And then I am revealed; I am unveiled.

I do not; will not take this gift lightly

It is my lover; my solace, my cave.

Words are the medium I use to express me

There is no greater method for me

To go inside,

To meditate

To be truly honest

Writing is my only outlet:

There is no other.

To Yourself Be True

One may try, not once, not twice
And often fail in their efforts
Sometimes it even goes without much labour
Trying to be someone else, doing other things.

Winds of circumstance blow one into foreign lands,
Where one is forced to be something else
Yet knowing all the while;
This is not where I belong.

Looking into the mirror and seeing a stranger
One's skin feels like a foreign article
Heavy and horrid and out of the elements
One carries it heavily, knowing well the awkwardness.

Daily haunted by ones spirit
The calling knocking persistently
Just that single voice, clearly beckoning;
Be who you really are; to yourself be true.

How Do I Pray?

Dear God,

I pray that my prayers are sufficient

That I do not offend your Holy presence

With unholy words, because of my unholy nature

I hope to use prayer to connect to God my Father

Not as a tool to make God a weapon

I acknowledge your mighty power

As well as your gentle kindness

Just help me remember Christ's words

When the disciples asked, Lord, teach us to pray;

Simply to say; "Our Father in heaven ..."

*Matthew 6:9-13

Where Am I?

Where am I?

I cannot find myself

Lost in a distant gaze

To where? To what? I know not.

Tear after tear they flow

Why am I crying?

Who is this person I am today?

Where is the contented me?

Where is the expectant, ready and willing me?

Oh, dear me, where on earth am I?

Soul weeping

There are times when you hurt physically:

You cry

Then there are times your soul pains:

You weep

Tears gush through open flood gates

Try as you might to understand

Nothing is revealed

When your soul is sick

It will seek earnestly for your mind

It will seek for you

It will dig deep and deeper than before

Until you get to the point of mourning

Drops of blood will replace those of sweat.

The heart will beat and tremble

The body will be at dis-ease

Nothing else flows but salt water

When the soul weeps

Amongst The Trees

It is as if each tree takes it all away

Each blade of grass absorbs it bit by bit

The misery I thought I had is lost in the rocks

The birds, crickets and buzzing bees

Sound away my loneliness

As if to say, "You have never been alone."

The gentle cool breeze refreshes my once resentful heart.

Gently breaking it wide open

The weight on my shoulders is chipped away

And I begin to wonder at the sight

Realizing that I was beginning to lose insight

Giving way to this great foresight

I may not know what it is yet but it is there

I may not see it yet but I choose to believe

I am of a purpose greater and bigger than I

My net-worth matters not as I sit amongst these trees

~The End~

Author Biography

Hannah H. Tarindwa defines herself as a Social Scientist and has been writing poetry ever since she was 13. She entered her first competition by virtue of being of the Budding Writers Association of Zimbabwe at age 14 on 40 words to describe poverty which she won and was made the youngest member of Artists Against Poverty. It was only when she was 17 that she started taking poetry somewhat seriously when she studied English Literature at Advanced level but she was not courageous enough to seek to be published. The poetry in this collection is from over seven years of writing. She has said that now that she has started publishing she intends on doing so at least twice a year for the rest of her life. Hannah feels that there aren't enough black African writers on the shelves of bookshops and hopes to change that scenario. She is also interested in Essay writing and is working on papers to be released within 2015 to 2016.

She lectures Journalism and Media and is currently based in Windhoek, Namibia.

www.ingramcontent.com/pod-product-compliance
Lightning Source LLC
Chambersburg PA
CBHW071842020426
42331CB00007B/1823